The North American Indians

The
Cherokee

Titles in The North American Indians series include:

The North American Indians

The
Cherokee

Catherine M. Petrini

KIDHAVEN
PRESS™

THOMSON
——— ✴ ———™
GALE

San Diego • Detroit • New York • San Francisco • Cleveland
New Haven, Conn. • Waterville, Maine • London • Munich

© 2004 by KidHaven Press. KidHaven Press is an imprint of The Gale Group, Inc.,
a division of Thomson Learning, Inc.

KidHaven™ and Thomson Learning™ are trademarks used herein under license.

For more information, contact
KidHaven Press
27500 Drake Rd.
Farmington Hills, MI 48331-3535
Or you can visit our Internet site at http://www.gale.com

LIBRARY OF CONGRESS CATALOGING-IN-PUBLICATION DATA

Petrini, Catherine M.
  The Cherokee / by Catherine M. Petrini.
    p. cm. — (North American Indians)
  Summary: Discusses the Cherokee people, their customs, family, organizations,
food gathering, religion, war, housing, and other aspects of daily life.
Includes bibliographical references and index.
  ISBN 0-7377-1511-1 (alk. paper)
    1. Cherokee Indians—Juvenile literature. [1. Cherokee Indians. 2. Indians of
North America—Southern states. 3. Indians of North America—Oklahoma.]
I. Title. II. Series.
  E99.C5P44 2004
  975.004'9755—dc21

                                                                    2003007309

Printed in China

Contents

Chapter One

The Mountaineers

A Cherokee legend says when the earth was new and its mud still soft, a huge bird called Great Turkey Buzzard flew low over the land. Where its wing tips swept the land upward, they formed mountains. This land of many mountains became the home of the Cherokee Indians. Today the area is known as the southern Appalachian highlands. It includes parts of North Carolina, South Carolina, Tennessee, Georgia, Kentucky, Alabama, Virginia, and West Virginia. These mountains, with their rugged terrain, cold winters, and many kinds of animals and plants, affected every part of Cherokee society. In fact, the Cherokee's lives were so closely linked to the high, rocky landscape that other tribes of the southeastern United States knew them as the Mountaineers.

Local Government

Most Cherokee lived in towns or villages located along streams or rivers. An average town had about 350 residents. Rocky terrain and steep mountain passes isolated these towns. So, for hundreds of years, the Cherokee did not have one tribal government to rule them all. Instead, each village made its own decisions about such issues as punishing wrongdoers or going to war.

The Cherokee were known as the Mountaineers because of their close ties to the Appalachian Mountains (pictured).

But the towns did have one important connection: the **clan** system. Every Cherokee belonged to one of seven clans, and each town contained members of every clan. Problems within a clan were solved by the clan's elders. Most disagreements between clans were handled by the town's chiefs and ruling councils.

To discuss issues that affected all the Cherokee, chiefs and other representatives of the towns sometimes met together in a central council. This council was mostly for sharing ideas. It could not tell people what to do.

By the late 1700s the structure of Cherokee government began to change. The need for trading with outsiders and for dealing as one tribe with the United States forced the Cherokee to create a central government. They elected a principal chief to preside over the Cherokee Nation as a whole. But towns still kept their own governments and solved their own people's problems.

Chiefs and Other Leaders

Every Cherokee town had two chiefs: the peace chief and the war chief. The peace chief ruled most of the time. The position was usually passed down through one clan; the older women of the peace chief's clan decided which clan member would be the next peace chief. Usually it was a man, but sometimes a woman was chosen. Because the color white stood for peace and happiness, the peace chief wore white and was often called the white chief.

During wars the war chief took over. Town residents voted to elect this chief, who was always a man. He wore red, the Cherokee color of success, and was also called the red chief.

Each chief was helped by several men. The two most important were the principal assistant and the

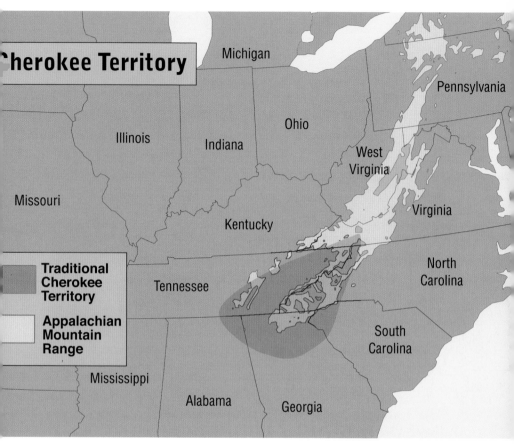

Cherokee Territory

Michigan

Pennsylvania

Ohio

Illinois

Indiana

West Virginia

Missouri

Virginia

Kentucky

Traditional Cherokee Territory

Appalachian Mountain Range

Tennessee

North Carolina

South Carolina

Mississippi

Alabama

Georgia

speaker. The principal assistant gave the chief advice and solved minor disputes among townspeople. The speaker was a priest. He talked about spiritual ideas and presided over religious ceremonies.

Each chief also had two councils of advisers. One council included a male representative from each clan. These men held court, made laws, and conducted religious ceremonies. The other was a council of Beloved Women, women who had fought bravely as warriors. The Beloved Women helped plan battle strategy and took part in religious ceremonies. They were also in charge of deciding what to do with prisoners of war. Some prisoners were tortured or killed by the Beloved Women. Some were kept as slaves or sold into slavery.

A Cherokee man and woman share a meal. The Cherokee valued freedom and human rights for all members of the tribe.

The luckiest ones were adopted into the village. They became Cherokee with the same rights as other towns-people.

Despite harsh treatment of some prisoners, the Cherokee valued human rights and individual freedom for all Cherokee. In town meetings every man and woman had the right to express opinions, no matter how unpopular. Good chiefs did not order people around. They considered all views and tried to make decisions almost everyone could agree with. Most Cherokee followed their chiefs because they respected them, not because they feared punishment. In fact, a person who disagreed with a decision usually was not bound by it. For example, if a town decided to go to war, a warrior who thought it was a bad idea was free to stay home.

Village Layout

When chiefs, councils, and townspeople had business to discuss, they met in the council house—a large, round building set on a mound of earth at the center of town. The council house was about fifty feet across. It contained just one room, big enough for the whole town to meet together. Seven thick wooden posts held up the center of the roof. These posts symbolized the seven clans. A hole in the center of the roof vented smoke from the building. Important officials sat on comfortable couches near the fire. Other people sat in rows of seats around the edges. Each clan sat together.

Cherokee gather in the center of the village.

The rest of the village surrounded the council house. Near the council house, a flat area was set aside for games, celebrations, and ceremonial dances. Towns had community fields for crops, family homes and gardens, and grain storehouses. Some towns also had **stockades** to protect people in case of enemy attacks.

Home and Hearth

In Cherokee families women owned the homes. Until about 1500 those homes were one-room pit houses about twenty feet square. The floor was dug into the ground. Mats of woven bark, reeds, or saplings formed walls. And wooden posts held up a **thatched** roof.

By around 1800 the Cherokee had learned to build more comfortable, practical houses. Most of these houses were square or rectangular. Some were log cabins, but others had walls made out of wooden planks. The Cherokee used a mixture of clay and grass to insulate these walls. The houses could have as many as three rooms and two stories. And some Cherokee even lived in large manor houses with glass windows and brick or stone fireplaces with chimneys.

Near each Cherokee home was a sweat house. This was a small, round house with no windows. A fire burned in the center to keep the temperature high. Family members sat inside this structure and sweated in the heat. They believed this could cure disease and purify their bodies for rituals and important life events.

Most Cherokee families also had a winter house, or hothouse. This small, round building was designed to keep people warm on very cold nights. The floor was set three or four feet into the ground. The earth around it helped keep the inside warm. Layers of wood and plaster formed the walls and cone-shaped roof. A hothouse had no windows and only a small hole in the top

Wooden posts hold up the thatched roof of this traditional Cherokee house.

to let smoke from the fire escape. The inside was so smoky that people wrapped their faces in woven cloth so they would not breathe too much smoke.

A Sense of Place

The hothouse was just one way the Cherokee **adapted** their lifestyle and living conditions to their surroundings. They saw themselves as part of their environment, so they tried to work with the climate and landscape rather than fighting against them. They created a culture that took advantage of their mountain homeland and preserved the landscape. Because they did, they survived and prospered for hundreds of years.

Chapter Two

Everyday Life

Every Cherokee man, woman, and child had a role to play in keeping their society running smoothly. Most Cherokee accepted these roles willingly. They believed the town was happier and healthier when people knew their places in it and did what they were supposed to.

Seven Clans

Cherokee society was matrilineal. That meant a child was born into the mother's clan and remained a member of that clan for life. Clan members, especially from different towns, might not know how they were related. Still they considered themselves to be close relatives.

A Cherokee's role in the village was closely tied to his or her clan. Each clan had its own way of doing things. Members of the Wolf Clan hunted like wolves, attacking their prey in packs. They also raised wolves and trained them like dogs. War chiefs came from this clan. The Deer Clan had the best deer hunters. They ran very fast, like deer. The Bird Clan raised crows and chicken hawks. They were skilled with **snares** and blowguns. The Red Paint Clan was thought to have great spiritual power. This Clan was named after a paint its members used in magic spells. Blue Clan members gathered a bluish plant called *saboni*, a narrow-leafed grass with berries that look like little cucumbers. They

The Cherokee believed that all tribe members had a role to play in society, as seen in this engraving of a Cherokee village hard at work.

used this plant for food and to make medicine to protect children from disease. The Wild Potato Clan gathered potatoes that grew along rivers and in swamps. During harsh winters people might have nothing to eat except these potatoes. And members of the Long Hair Clan wore elaborate, twisted hairstyles and walked with a proud, twisting motion of their shoulders. Peace chiefs came from the Long Hair Clan.

The clan system had rules. People of the same clan could not marry each other. When a couple married they moved into the home of the bride's mother or started their own household. Nobody with a clan was ever homeless. A divorced man, or anyone with nowhere else to go, could always move in with clan members. Children belonged to their mother's clan, and fathers had no custody rights.

Growing Food

The jobs clan members did depended on whether they were male or female. Women and girls were in charge of growing, gathering, and preparing food. In addition, some women did jobs that were considered men's work, such as hunting or fighting in wars. But even a skilled huntress or female warrior could not hunt or fight full-time. Farming came first. It was a woman's most important job.

Women worked together in the town's fields to grow corn, beans, squash, and other crops. In addition, women and girls of each household tended a family garden. They also ventured into the forests and swamps outside of town to gather nuts, berries, potatoes, mushrooms, and other foods that grew wild. Many women worked while carrying babies in slings on their backs. Girls learned by watching and helping their mothers, grandmothers, and aunts.

Corn was the main food in the Cherokee diet. Cherokee families ate it nearly every day. Sometimes they ate plain corn, but usually they ate cornbread. They also made corn dumplings, soup, and mush. They even used corn to make a sour drink that could be served hot or cold.

Women were in charge of cooking the corn and other foods. But they did not make three separate meals a day. Instead, women always kept food ready for family members to eat whenever they felt hungry.

When they were not feeding their families, women tended animals and made things their families needed. They tanned hides and wove cloth. They also made household tools. Women wove reeds into beautiful, watertight baskets. And they molded clay into pots.

A Cherokee woman weaves reeds (below) into a watertight basket (left).

Women also took care of and disciplined children. The Cherokee did not believe in spanking children. In fact, they rarely punished them at all. Children learned how they were supposed to act by watching adults and listening to stories and instructions. Those who misbehaved were teased or ignored until they did what was expected.

The Hunt

Men were in charge of hunting and fishing. A boy learned these skills from his mother's brothers, other clansmen, or his father. Groups of hunters stayed away from the village for weeks looking for game. The Cherokee hunted deer using bows and arrows or spears. They used blowguns to kill smaller animals, including rabbits, groundhogs, squirrels, and birds. Blowguns were hollowed-out pieces of river **cane** rubbed smooth. The hunter slipped a wood-

A Cherokee hunter uses a blowgun (right) to shoot wooden darts (below) at small prey.

en dart into the tube. Then he held the tube to his lips and blew quickly and forcefully to shoot out the dart. A Cherokee boy had to prove his skill with a blowgun before he was allowed to hunt with a bow and arrow.

Men and boys also caught fish to eat. Sometimes they fished with a hook carved from bone and tied to a fishing line. Other times they speared fish or caught them in box traps. They also fished by damming a stream to create a pond. Then they poured chestnut juice into the water. The juice put the fish to sleep. Then boys waded in and pulled out some of the sleeping fish. Afterward they knocked down the dam. Water rushed in and woke the rest of the fish, which swam away unharmed.

War Parties

Men were also the warriors of the tribe. War played a major role in Cherokee life. Usually fighting was done by war parties. Most war parties had about ten warriors, but some had only two or three. War parties usually made quick, violent raids rather than fighting full-blown battles.

The most common reason for fighting was to **avenge** a murder. When a Cherokee was killed, the victim's clan members were duty bound to avenge the death. To do that they had to kill the killer or a member of the killer's clan or village.

Other wars erupted over hunting rights or land disputes. In these battles the Cherokee's greatest enemies were the Choctaw and Creek. But they also fought the Chickasaw, Shawnee, and Seneca.

Cherokee warriors liked to catch their enemies by surprise so they traveled swiftly and quietly in single file. They communicated with bird calls and other animal sounds. And anyone who stepped on a twig and broke it had to carry it in his hand for the rest of the day so he would remember to walk carefully.

Fun and Games

When they were not working or fighting, Cherokee children and adults amused themselves with games, sports, and other kinds of fun. The most popular team sport was called *anetsa,* which meant "little brother to war." The game was similar to lacrosse. Men played using short sticks with baskets attached; women played with their hands. Teams earned points by throwing the ball through a goal made of sticks driven into the ground.

Sometimes the men from a town faced the women in a friendly match. Other times teams of men from two towns played each other. In these matches as many as fifty people might play on a team. The game was rough, even violent. Players could be injured or killed trying to stop their opponents from scoring.

Cherokee men and women prepare for a friendly game of *anetsa.*

Cherokee women use sticks with baskets to play a game of *anetsa*.

A safer activity was storytelling. Children listened while adults told stories. Some were stories about Cherokee history and legends; others were new stories that taught traditional values. Stories could be either funny or serious. But they all helped families pass the long winter nights. More importantly, they tied Cherokee families and clans together by handing down a set of beliefs from generation to generation.

Chapter Three

Spiritual Beliefs and Practices

Religion was a part of all the Cherokee's activities. Their beliefs centered on the ideas that everything in the world was connected and that everything was important. To the Cherokee the universe was in balance when opposites (such as men and women, or animals and plants) were held in equal respect, with neither considered above the other.

Sometimes people forgot those things and threw the world out of balance. For example, a hunter might kill an animal that was not needed for food or clothing. The Cherokee believed such an act could cause sickness, bad weather, or failed crops. As a result the purpose of many religious rituals was to restore balance, bringing back health and prosperity. Other rituals gave thanks or purified people's minds and bodies for certain life events.

The Power of Names

The Cherokee believed a person's name had spiritual power. A name was not just a title but part of who someone was. On either the fourth or seventh day after a child's birth, the village held a naming ceremony. Some children were named after an animal or object they looked like. A boy who resembled a deer might be called Buck. Other names referred to something that happened at the moment of birth. A child born during a storm might be named Rain Falling. After contact with whites many Cherokee gave their children European names, but they gave them traditional Cherokee names too.

As Cherokee grew and changed, their names changed with them. They were renamed for personal traits or earned names by doing something memorable. For example, one Cherokee chief had a name that translated into English as He Keeps Falling Over. This man once tried to talk to U.S. president Andrew Jackson to ask him to stop the government from taking Cherokee land. When he returned home, he told his friends he had failed. So his name became He Tried But Failed.

A Cherokee woman poses for a photo in the Appalachian mountains.

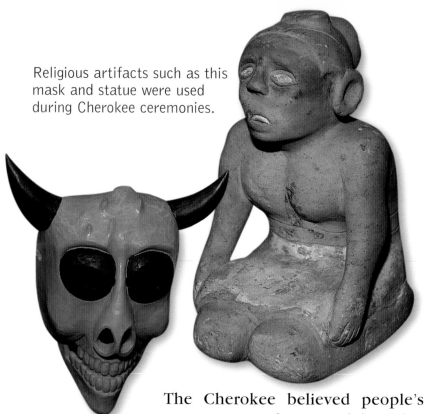

Religious artifacts such as this mask and statue were used during Cherokee ceremonies.

The Cherokee believed people's names were so much a part of them that a name could get sick, just like any other body part. If herbs and healing rituals did not cure a disease, the healer might decide it was the patient's name that was ill. To cure the illness a priest gave the patient a new name.

Selection and Training of Priests

To the Cherokee, powers of healing and spirituality were part of the same thing. Both were called "medicine." People who knew medicine were called medicine men and women.

Medicine people who held positions in the town government were called priests. Priests were always men. They led official ceremonies and healed sick people with prayers and rituals. The priesthood usually ran in families.

A baby boy who was meant to be a priest was called a "devoted son." His formal training began when he was

A Cherokee dancer performs a traditional dance during a prayer ceremony.

nine or ten. An older priest took him away from the village for eight days. On the first day they waited on a mountaintop for sunrise. The boy watched the horizon for the sun's first rays. Once the sun peeked out, he had to follow it with his eyes all day until sunset. He could not look away even once. If he did his training ended and he was no longer a devoted son.

If he passed the first test, his training continued. For the next seven days, the priest taught him about Cherokee beliefs and rituals. The priest also showed him how to use a divining crystal. Divining crystals were special quartz crystals that the Cherokee believed could predict the future or find lost objects. Only a person with special training could use them.

Other Medicine Men and Women

Priests were not the only people with spiritual powers. Sometimes a boy or girl was raised to be another kind of medicine man or woman. Twins, or babies who were born during an unusual event like an earthquake or comet sighting, were expected to be special. When they were older they might become **apprentices** to village medicine people. Some of these special children were thought to be visionaries or prophets, people who saw the future in dreams or visions. Others learned to make love spells or to use prayers and charms to cure illness.

Cherokee medicine men like Swimmer (pictured) conducted rituals and ceremonies.

As these children grew they spent a lot of time alone in the woods. That was supposed to give them a chance to talk with spiritual beings known as the Little People. This was a legendary race of people who grew to be about three feet tall. The Cherokee believed the Little People were their teachers, guides, and guardians. The Little People were also said to be full of mischief. They played tricks on those who did not respect them.

Only disrespectful people had to fear the Little People. But even good people were afraid of witches. The Cherokee believed that some people who knew medicine used it in evil ways, casting spells to make others sick. If a patient's sickness was thought to be caused by a witch, the healer made a new spell to fight against the witch's evil one.

People who were not professional medicine men and women could be healers too. In fact, many women were skilled in the use of herbs and other plants. Often a sick person's mother or another female clan member tried to cure the illness with herbal medicine. If the cure did not work, the family would call a priest or medicine person.

Green Corn Festival

Each year the Cherokee celebrated seven major religious festivals. The most important was the Green Corn Festival. This happened in the summer when the first corn ripened. The main point of the festival was to give thanks for the corn crop and to honor the corn spirit, Selu, who was believed to be the first Cherokee woman.

Each town had its own customs for the Green Corn Festival, but some of the rituals were the same everywhere. The festival usually lasted from three to seven days. Before it started women cleaned their houses.

Men cleaned the council house and other public areas. Then, after a ritual **fast**, anyone who owed a debt or had committed a crime (except murder) came forward to be forgiven. And the priest reminded the town's women of their duty to grow corn.

During the rest of the festival, people visited with friends and relatives, ate special foods, sang, and danced. A priest led the warriors and Beloved Women in a ceremonial dance. While they danced he shook a rattle made out of a gourd filled with gravel. Other people could take part in other festival dances. They sang sacred songs and played music while they danced. Some shook rattles tied to their legs. Others played red drums or wooden flutes.

A Cherokee man leads a tour through a council house (below), where priests held religious ceremonies (left) and tribal meetings.

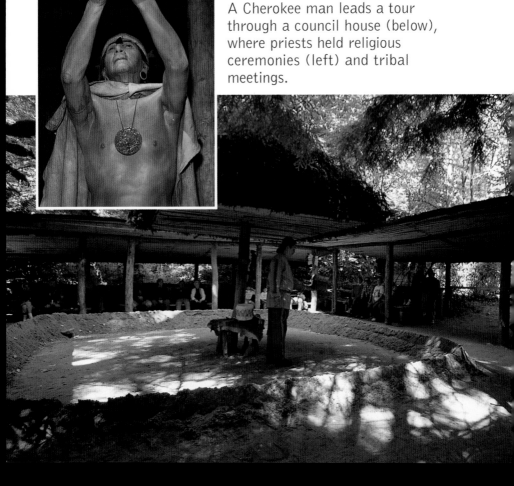

Cherokee dancers use rattles during a religious ritual.

Arrival of the Missionaries

The Cherokee continued to celebrate their festivals even after the first Christian missionaries arrived around 1800. The missionaries started schools to teach Cherokee boys and girls to read and write in English. Some missionaries taught adults too. They taught reading so the Cherokee could read the Bible. Few Cherokee were interested in the Bible at first. But some did want to read and write in English. With more white

Cherokee children pose in front of their schoolhouse.
Christian missionaries started such schools to teach English
to Cherokee children.

people living close by, it seemed important to know
how.

At some mission schools students were also taught
to dress and act like white children. The Cherokee did
not like this. They wanted their children to remember
their own heritage. Eventually some Cherokee did
become Christians, but almost all of them kept their
own beliefs too.

Mission schools were only one sign of changes to
come. Only a few decades after the arrival of Christian
missionaries, the traditional Cherokee way of life would
be swept away forever.

Chapter Four

Endings and Beginnings

After the American Revolution, the Cherokee's world was controlled more and more by the federal and state governments of the United States. The Cherokee did their best to survive in this changing world and to live in peace with the new settlers. Many learned English, started businesses to trade with whites, wove and wore fabric instead of deerskin, and learned to hunt with rifles. In the end, though, their way of life was taken from them anyway.

A Written Language

The most important idea the Cherokee adopted from whites was a written language. In 1809 only a few Cherokee had learned to read and write in English. That year a Cherokee named Sequoya came up with an idea. He thought his people would be able to communicate among themselves more easily if they could write their own language. He became the first person to create a written language by himself to be used by a whole society. It took many years for Sequoya to finish. But in 1821 he finally did. Then he taught his daughter to read and write in Cherokee. When his people saw that even

Sequoya (pictured) took more than twelve years to create a written Cherokee language.

The Cherokee alphabet (above) has eighty-five symbols.
Sequoya designed the written language to be easy to learn.

a child could read his language, everyone wanted to learn. Soon almost every Cherokee could read and write in this new language.

A few years later the Cherokee started publishing their own newspaper, the *Cherokee Phoenix*. Articles were printed in Cherokee and English. Sequoya's invention, and the newspaper that made use of it, helped the Cherokee to keep informed and to fight for their rights during the struggle that was to follow.

Broken Promises

Since the early 1700s European settlers, and then the U.S. government, had wanted the Cherokee's land. The Cherokee sold them some in a series of treaties and other deals. When the Cherokee refused to sell more, the U.S. Army attacked them. That forced them to give up even more property. In return, the government promised to protect them from losing any more of their land. That promise would be broken again and again.

Between 1812 and 1814, the United States battled both British soldiers and Creek warriors. The Cherokee sided with the Americans. Many Cherokee fought bravely under the command of U.S. general Andrew Jackson. When a Cherokee chief saved Jackson's life, the general swore he

Although Cherokee chief John Ross (left) convinced the U.S. Supreme Court to protect Cherokee lands, President Andrew Jackson (right) refused to enforce the Court's decision.

would always be a friend to the Cherokee. In 1828 Jackson was elected president and quickly forgot his vow.

Another event of 1828 changed the Cherokee's lives forever: Gold was discovered in Georgia, in the heart of the Cherokee Nation. Georgians wanted the gold for themselves. So the state passed laws against the Cherokee. It became illegal for Cherokee to mine gold on their own land. It was illegal for one Cherokee to discourage another from selling land to whites. The Cherokee could not speak as witnesses in trials against white people. Then the state of Georgia divided up the Cherokee land and began selling it.

By this time the Cherokee had their own central government. John Ross, the principal chief, traveled to Washington, D.C., to fight for his people. Eventually he won. The U.S. Supreme Court sided with the Cherokee, saying it was illegal for Georgia or any other state to take their land. But President Jackson refused to enforce the decision.

Then, about a hundred wealthy Cherokee men decided that all the Cherokee should give up their land to the whites. In 1835 they signed a treaty with the U.S. government agreeing to sell all Cherokee land and move west. This treaty was illegal. The men were not elected by the Cherokee and did not have the right to speak for the tribe. But the treaty became law anyway. The government said the Cherokee had until 1838 to move to Indian Territory, an area that later became the state of Oklahoma.

The Trail of Tears

A few Cherokee gave up right away and moved west. But most stayed. For three years they tried to convince the U.S. government to let them keep their homeland. But in May 1838 soldiers began arresting Cherokee families

Trail of Tears Routes

Legend:
- ▪ ▪ ▪ ▪ Land Route
- ——— Water Route
- ——— Other Major Routes
- ● City En Route

and removing them from their homes. The Cherokee were allowed to bring almost nothing but the clothes they were wearing. Those who moved too slowly were prodded with **bayonets**. Many families were separated. In all, about seventeen thousand Cherokee were captured. The only free Cherokee left in the East were about a thousand who hid in the mountains.

The soldiers kept the captives in **stokade** camps. The camps had no shelter and little clothing or bedding. The army provided some food and water but not enough. And the foods were kinds the Cherokee were not used to and did not know how to cook, like wheat flour instead of cornmeal. The poor conditions made people sick. Many died before leaving for Indian Territory.

When it was time to go, groups of Cherokee were led west along several routes. Some of the first groups were taken by river in large **flatboats**. But the boats were too crowded. Some people fell overboard and drowned. Others got sick and died. After that the army decided the rest would go by land.

The land route was dangerous too. There were only enough wagons to carry supplies, so most of the Cherokee had to walk the twelve hundred miles to Indian Territory. Most of them were barefoot, there was not enough food, and the weather was bad. Thousands of people got sick, especially older people and babies.

It took more than four months to reach Indian Territory. By then more than four thousand Cherokee had died in the camps or along the trail. The Cherokee call their journey the Trail Where They Cried, or the Trail of Tears.

A New Life in the West

Arriving in Indian Territory did not end the ordeal. Supplies promised by the government never arrived. The landscape was different from what the Cherokee were used to, and they did not know how to make a living from it. Also, the Cherokee who had moved earlier did not want the newcomers to be in charge—even though the elected officials of the Cherokee Nation, including Principal Chief Ross, were in the new group.

Many people blamed their suffering on the men who signed the illegal treaty. In June 1839 some of those men were murdered. But Ross and other leaders worked to help everyone live together peacefully.

In the West the Cherokee did what they had always done: adapted and survived. They created a single government to unite them. They learned how to farm there, and they built a capital city called Tahlequah in what is now eastern Oklahoma. They started schools for their children and published a new newspaper, the *Cherokee Advocate.* Once again the Cherokee Nation prospered and grew.

The Cherokee nation, based in eastern Oklahoma (above), has more than two hundred thousand members.

The Cherokee Today

Today's Cherokee Nation, still based in Tahlequah, has more than two hundred thousand members. They are called the Western Cherokee. There is also a Cherokee reservation in North Carolina. The twelve thousand people there are called the Eastern Band of the Cherokee. They are descended from those who hid from the soldiers.

Through all of their suffering and the loss of their homeland, the Cherokee have managed to survive and thrive. They have done it by adapting some of their customs to modern demands. At the same time they have clung to the beliefs and traditions that make them who they are. Although the Mountaineers were torn away from their mountains, the lessons they learned there are still a part of the Cherokee people.

Glossary

adapt: To make changes in order to do better in a particular place or situation. An adaptation is a change that is made for that reason.

apprentice: A young person who learns the skills for a certain kind of work by watching and helping an expert.

avenge: To get justice by punishing someone who has done wrong.

bayonet: A steel blade attached to the end of a soldier's rifle and used to stab an enemy.

cane: A kind of tall, woody grass or reed that has hollow, flexible stems and often grows along riverbanks.

clan: A group of people who are all related, some distantly, as part of the same extended family.

fast: An extended time during which a person chooses not to eat, sometimes as part of a religious ritual.

flatboat: A boat with a flat bottom and square ends, sometimes called a barge; it is usually used for transporting freight in shallow water, such as a river.

snare: A trap used for catching birds or small animals.

stockade: An enclosure or pen with high walls, used either for protecting people against enemies or for holding them as prisoners.

thatch: Roofing material made of thick clumps of grass, reeds, or strips of bark attached to a wooden framework.

For Further Exploration

Books

Alex W. Bealer, *Only the Names Remain: The Cherokees and the Trail of Tears.* Boston: Little, Brown, 1996. This classic history of the Cherokee Indians, recently reprinted, traces the evolution of their culture, beginning before first contact with Europeans and concluding with the Trail of Tears. Includes an index.

Joseph Bruchac, *The Trail of Tears.* New York: Random House, 1999. The author uses Cherokee principal chief John Ross as the focus for this well-researched study of the Cherokee's forced migration West, with flashbacks to events leading up to the move. A "Step Into Reading" book, aimed at grade levels two to four.

Elaine Landau, *The Cherokees.* New York: Franklin Watts, 1992. This overview of the Cherokee's history, customs, and current situation is vividly illustrated with photographs, drawings, and maps. Includes a glossary, index, and resource list.

Lynn King Lossiah, *The Secrets and Mysteries of the Cherokee Little People: Yunwi Tsunsdi.* Cherokee: Cherokee, 1998. A collection of stories and legends about the mythical Little People who were said to be protectors and teachers of the Cherokee.

Marcelina Reed, *Seven Clans of the Cherokee Society.* Cherokee: Cherokee, 1993. A brief description of the Cherokee clan system.

Peter Roop and Connie Roop, *If You Lived with the Cherokee.* New York: Scholastic, 1998. Each brief chapter in this illustrated and richly detailed study asks and then answers a question about what it was like to grow up in a Cherokee village, focusing mostly on the time before the relocation West.

R. Conrad Stein, *The Trail of Tears.* Chicago: Childrens, 1993 (revised edition). A detailed history of Cherokee relations with the United States government, culminating in the Cherokee's relocation. Contains many photographs, maps, and drawings, as well as an index. Part of the "Cornerstones of Freedom" series.

Thomas Bryan Underwood, ed., *Cherokee Legends and the Trail of Tears.* Cherokee: Cherokee, 1993. This collection of Cherokee folklore is supplemented by an account of the Trail of Tears that was written in 1890 by an army private who helped with the Cherokee removal. The combination of traditional animal tales with the harrowing narrative is jarring, but both parts of the book are fascinating.

Evelyn Wolfson, *From Abenaki to Zuni: A Dictionary of Native American Tribes.* New York: Walker, 1988. Entries on sixty-eight North American tribes are arranged alphabetically and include information on location, culture, history, and beliefs. Includes a glossary, bibliography, and index.

Websites

Cherokee Nation (www.cherokee.org). One of the most comprehensive and reliable sites for Cherokee-related information, this is the official site of the Cherokee Nation. Along with news from the Nation and information on its current government, it includes dozens of articles on Cherokee culture and history, and even recipes. In an effort to preserve and teach the Cherokee language, the site provides language lessons with sound files and a free, downloadable type font of Cherokee characters.

Cherokee Phoenix (http://blueotter.addr.com). This site of the bilingual *Cherokee Phoenix* newspaper, which was published from 1828 to 1834, presents complete transcripts of articles from the 1828–1830 issues, with other issues to be added. The site also includes historical photos and maps, articles on Cherokee history, and resources for learning the Cherokee language, including a tutorial.

Museum of the Cherokee Indian (www.cherokeemuseum.org). The official website of the Cherokee, North Carolina, museum provides an overview of the museum's collections and archives. It includes a detailed, annotated map of the Trail of Tears routes, frequently asked questions and little-known facts about the Cherokee, a list of resources, and museum visitor information.

Say Hello in Cherokee (www.ipl.org). Run by the University of Michigan's School of Information, the Internet Public Library's "Kidspace" includes a page on the language, culture, and history of the Cherokee. It centers around a lesson on saying "hello" in Cherokee and includes sound files for listening to the language.

Western Cherokee Nation (www.westerncherokee nation. org). The official site of the Western Cherokee Nation lists tribal leaders and other current information about today's Cherokee, and includes a section on traditional lore, history, culture, and laws.

Index

Picture Credits

Cover: © Bettmann/CORBIS
© Bettmann/CORBIS, 17, 23
© Blackbirch Press, 9, 34 (right), 38
© Jay Dickman/CORBIS, 7
© Kevin Fleming/CORBIS, 38 (inset)
Library of Congress, 33
© Museum of the Cherokee, 18 (top)
© Nativestock.com, 17 (inset), 18, 20, 21, 24 (both), 25, 26, 28 (both), 30, 34 (left)
© NorthWind Picture Archives, 10, 11, 15, 29
© Charles Banks Wilson/Blackbirch Press, 32

About the Author

Catherine M. Petrini has written twenty young-adult novels, under pseudonyms, for "Sweet Valley High" and other teen series. Titles include *Wanted for Murder, A Stranger in the House, Mystery Date, Earthquake,* and a historical-fiction saga, *The Patmans of Sweet Valley.* A former magazine editor, she is also the coauthor of a nonfiction book called *Opportunities in Training and Development Careers.* Her most recent book, *The Italian Americans,* was published in 2002 by Lucent Books.

Petrini is a frequent speaker on writing-related topics, and also hosts a radio show. She has a bachelor's degree in English from the University of Virginia and a master's degree in writing from Johns Hopkins University.

A longtime admirer of Cherokee culture, she has researched and driven the twelve-hundred-mile route of the Trail of Tears.